TAMPA BAY LIGHTNING

BY BRENDAN FLYNN

Copyright © 2023 by Press Room Editions. All rights reserved. No part of this book may be used or reproduced in any manner whatsoever, including internet usage, without written permission from the copyright owner, except in the case of brief quotations embodied in critical articles and reviews.

Book design by Maggie Villaume
Cover design by Maggie Villaume

Photographs ©: Nick Wass/AP Images, cover; Andrew Bershaw/Icon Sportswire, 4–5, 9, 23, 28; David Rosenblum/Icon Sportswire, 7; CHO/AP Images, 10–11; Chris O'Meara/AP Images, 13; IHA/Icon Sportswire, 14–15; Andy Mead/Icon Sportswire, 16–17; Ryan Remiorz/The Canadian Press/AP Images, 19; Cliff Welch/Icon Sportswire, 21; Mark LoMoglio/Icon Sportswire, 24–25; Jason Franson/The Canadian Press/AP Images, 27

Press Box Books, an imprint of Press Room Editions.

ISBN
978-1-63494-497-7 (library bound)
978-1-63494-523-3 (paperback)
978-1-63494-574-5 (epub)
978-1-63494-549-3 (hosted ebook)

Library of Congress Control Number: 2022902463

Distributed by North Star Editions, Inc.
2297 Waters Drive
Mendota Heights, MN 55120
www.northstareditions.com

Printed in the United States of America
082022

ABOUT THE AUTHOR

Brendan Flynn is a San Francisco resident and an author of numerous children's books. In addition to writing about sports, Flynn also enjoys competing in triathlons, Scrabble tournaments, and chili cook-offs.

TABLE OF CONTENTS

CHAPTER 1
HOMETOWN HEROES
5

CHAPTER 2
ICE SKATES AND PALM TREES
11

CHAPTER 3
RAISING THE CUP
17

SUPERSTAR PROFILE
STEVEN STAMKOS
22

CHAPTER 4
BACK-TO-BACK CHAMPS
25

QUICK STATS	30
GLOSSARY	31
TO LEARN MORE	32
INDEX	32

1

Mathieu Joseph of the Tampa Bay Lightning takes a shot during Game 5 of the 2021 Stanley Cup Final.

HOMETOWN HEROES

The scene at Amalie Arena in Tampa, Florida, was electric. The Tampa Bay Lightning clung to a 1–0 lead against the Montreal Canadiens. It was Game 5 of the 2021 Stanley Cup Final. Fans screamed and cheered as the clock ran down.

A year earlier, the same arena had sat empty as the Lightning won the Cup. The National Hockey League (NHL) season had paused in March 2020. COVID-19 was spreading through North America. When teams began playing again, no fans were allowed in the arenas.

In 2021, the Lightning wanted to win the Stanley Cup again in front of a full crowd. The series opened with two easy home victories for Tampa Bay. The Lightning also took Game 3 in Montreal, Quebec. They were just one win away from a sweep and a second straight title. But the Canadiens won Game 4 in overtime.

Game 5 was another close game. Tampa Bay took a 1–0 lead late in the second period. Ross Colton scored off a perfect setup from David Savard. But the

Ross Colton (79) scores against the Montreal Canadiens during Game 5 of the 2021 Stanley Cup Final.

Canadiens goalie was tough. He didn't allow another goal. It was up to Tampa Bay goalie Andrei Vasilevskiy to finish the job.

Early in the third period, Vasilevskiy stuffed Montreal's Josh Anderson on a breakaway. Vasilevskiy saved two more shots in the middle of the third. Montreal kept pressing hard. Then, in the last 30 seconds, the Canadiens had their final chance. But Tampa Bay's Yanni Gourde cleared the puck down the ice, and the clock ran out.

Vasilevskiy was mobbed by his teammates. The cheers of the Tampa crowd shook the rafters. The Lightning had won their second straight Stanley Cup. And this time, they did it in front of their adoring fans.

CONN SMYTHE TROPHY

The Conn Smythe Trophy is awarded to the most valuable player of the Stanley Cup playoffs. In 2021, Vasilevskiy won the award. He was in the net for every one of the Lightning's 23 playoff games that year. He allowed just 1.90 goals per game and posted five shutouts.

Lightning goalie Andrei Vasilevskiy hoists the Stanley Cup after winning the 2021 championship.

2

Phil Esposito (right) cuts the ribbon to celebrate the founding of the Tampa Bay Lightning.

ICE SKATES AND PALM TREES

In 1990, a business group wanted to put an expansion team in Tampa-St. Petersburg, Florida. Hall of Famer Phil Esposito led the way. The group knew it needed to show that enough hockey fans lived in the area.

That September, the group staged an exhibition game. The Los Angeles Kings played against the Pittsburgh Penguins. The game took place at a large baseball stadium in St. Petersburg. A crowd of 25,581 people showed up. It was the largest crowd ever to watch an NHL game.

The turnout was enough to convince the league. Esposito's group got the rights to form a new NHL team. The Tampa Bay Lightning began playing in the 1992–93 season.

Most expansion teams aren't very good at first. The Lightning were no

MAKING HISTORY

In 1992, Manon Rhéaume became a household name in hockey circles. She was the first woman ever to play in an NHL game. The Lightning brought the 20-year-old goalie to their first training camp. She played in an exhibition game on September 23. Rhéaume went on to compete with the Canadian women's hockey team. She helped the team win a silver medal at the 1998 Winter Olympics.

exception. They made the playoffs just once in their first 10 years. Even so, their first game was one to remember.

On October 7, 1992, the Lightning hosted the Chicago Blackhawks. The home team exploded for five goals in the first period. Chris Kontos scored the first two goals in Lightning history. He added two more in the second period. Tampa Bay rolled to a 7–3 victory.

Goalie Manon Rhéaume gets ready to start during a 1992 exhibition game with the Lightning.

The early years were lean ones, however. The Lightning's first All-Star was Brian Bradley. The center scored 42 goals in Tampa Bay's first season. Defenseman Roman Hamrlik was the team's first draft pick. He spent most of his first six NHL seasons with Tampa Bay.

The team's first true star arrived in 1998. Tampa Bay picked Vincent Lecavalier first overall in the 1998 draft. The center was just 18 years old. Lecavalier spent 14 seasons with the Lightning. He played a big role in turning the expansion team into champions.

Vincent Lecavalier handles the puck during a 2000 game.

Cory Stillman advances the puck down the ice during a 2004 game.

RAISING
THE CUP

The Lightning hired John Tortorella as their head coach in January 2001. He was a fierce competitor and got results. In 2003–04, the Lightning posted the best record in the Eastern Conference.

That team was loaded with talent. Martin St. Louis led the Lightning with 38 goals and 56 assists. Vincent Lecavalier, Cory Stillman, and Brad Richards helped share the scoring load. Veteran forward Dave Andreychuk provided grit and leadership. And Nikolai Khabibulin was solid in the net.

The Lightning cruised through the first two rounds of the 2004 playoffs. Then the Philadelphia Flyers gave them a battle in the Eastern Conference Final. The series stretched to seven games. But Tampa Bay pulled out a 2–1 victory in Game 7.

The Lightning then faced the Calgary Flames in the Stanley Cup Final. It was another close series. Game 6 went to double overtime. St. Louis scored to send the Lightning to Game 7. Back in Florida, Ruslan Fedotenko scored twice, and the Lightning won 2–1. In just their 12th

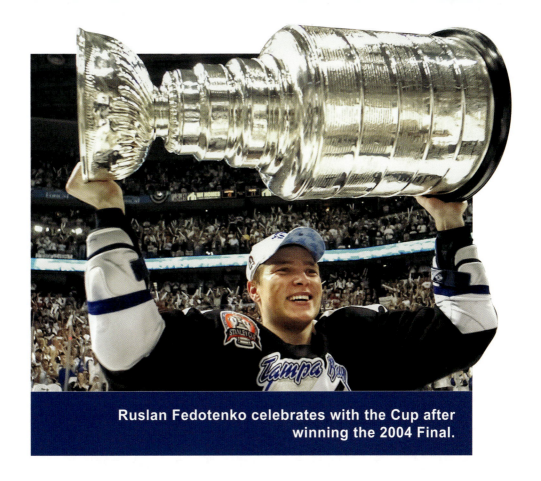

Ruslan Fedotenko celebrates with the Cup after winning the 2004 Final.

season, the Lightning were Stanley Cup champions!

That success didn't last, however. In the next two seasons, the Lightning were knocked out of the playoffs in the first round. Between 2008 and 2013, they made the playoffs just once.

Things turned around in 2014–15. That season, a group of exciting young forwards emerged as stars. Centers Steven Stamkos and Tyler Johnson tied for the team lead with 72 points. Right wing Nikita Kucherov scored 29 goals. Left wing Ondrej Palat had a team-high 47 assists. And they were all under 25 years old.

The Lightning returned to the Stanley Cup Final in 2015. This time, they lost to Chicago in six games. In 2017–18 and 2018–19, the Lightning dominated the

> **THE BOLTS**
>
> Lightning fans have referred to the team as "the Bolts" for years. The team's jerseys have always featured a lightning bolt on the front. In 2008, the team added a third jersey. It had just the word "BOLTS" across the players' chests.

Martin St. Louis wears the "BOLTS" jersey during a 2011 game.

regular season. However, they couldn't keep it up in the playoffs. Fans wondered whether the Lightning would ever win another Cup. That question would soon be answered.

SUPERSTAR PROFILE

STEVEN STAMKOS

Steven Stamkos burst onto the NHL scene in his second season. Tampa Bay made Stamkos the first overall pick of the 2008 NHL Draft. In 2009–10, he led the NHL with 51 goals. Two years later, he led the league again. This time, he scored a career-high 60 goals. He was especially strong on the power play. Stamkos often camped out in the face-off circle. Then he used his deadly slap shot to torment opposing goalies.

Stamkos showed his toughness, too. He battled back from many injuries over his career. He even broke his leg in 2013. The Lightning saw his hard work. They named Stamkos captain in 2014. He added leadership to his scoring duties. Stamkos proved he could handle both tasks. He scored 45 goals in 2018–19. Then he captained the Lightning to Stanley Cup titles the next two

Steven Stamkos takes control during a 2020 game against the Los Angeles Kings.

4

Nikita Kucherov skates down the ice during a 2020 game.

BACK-TO-BACK CHAMPS

In 2019–20, the Lightning were on a roll. Nikita Kucherov and Steven Stamkos were lighting up the scoreboard. Meanwhile, Andrei Vasilevskiy had emerged as one of the NHL's top goalies. Tampa Bay was battling with the Boston Bruins for first place in the Atlantic Division.

Then in March 2020, COVID-19 ground the season to a halt. When play resumed in August, the league skipped right to the playoffs. The Lightning made quick work of Columbus and Boston in the first two rounds. Then they faced the New York Islanders in the conference final. They won three of the first five games. In Game 6, Anthony Cirelli scored in overtime to clinch the series. Tampa Bay was finally back in the Stanley Cup Final.

The Dallas Stars proved to be no match for the Lightning. Vasilevskiy's

PLAYING IN THE BUBBLE

COVID-19 made the NHL playoffs in 2020 unlike any other. Playoff teams played and practiced in a "bubble." Players couldn't go home during the playoffs. They didn't see anyone outside the league. When the Lightning won the Cup, the players were happy for two reasons. One was the championship. The other was going home for the first time in months.

Andrei Vasilevskiy made 22 saves in his Game 6 shutout during the 2020 Stanley Cup Final.

shutout in Game 6 gave Tampa Bay a 2–0 win and its second Stanley Cup title.

The Lightning started out hot in the 2020–21 season. But they had a late-season slump. That knocked them into third place in the Central Division.

Victor Hedman blasts a slap shot during a 2021 game against the St. Louis Blues.

Even so, Tampa Bay was ready to play when the playoffs rolled around.

First, the Lightning defeated their rivals, the Florida Panthers, in six games. Then they took out the Carolina

Hurricanes in five games. That set up a rematch with the Islanders in the semifinal.

It was a tense series. The teams split the first six games. In Game 7, Tampa Bay's Yanni Gourde scored a shorthanded goal in the second period. Vasilevskiy closed the series with another shutout. The 1–0 victory sent Tampa Bay back to the Stanley Cup Final. There, the Lightning took care of business against the Canadiens.

In the 2021–22 season, Stamkos, Victor Hedman, and Vasilevskiy were still going strong. Tampa Bay fans hoped the Lightning would stay Stanley Cup contenders for years to come.

TAMPA BAY LIGHTNING
QUICK STATS

FOUNDED: 1992

STANLEY CUP CHAMPIONSHIPS: 3 (2004, 2020, 2021)

KEY COACHES:

- Terry Crisp (1992–97): 142 wins, 204 losses, 45 ties

- John Tortorella (2001–08): 239 wins, 222 losses, 36 ties, 38 overtime losses

- Jon Cooper (2013–): 384 wins, 197 losses, 53 overtime losses

HOME ARENA: Amalie Arena (Tampa, FL)

MOST CAREER POINTS: Martin St. Louis (953)

MOST CAREER GOALS: Steven Stamkos (439)

MOST CAREER ASSISTS: Martin St. Louis (588)

MOST CAREER SHUTOUTS: Andrei Vasilevskiy (26)

*Stats are accurate through the 2020–21 season.

GLOSSARY

ASSISTS
Passes, rebounds, or deflections that result in goals.

BREAKAWAY
When a player has a clear path to the net with no defenders between them and the goalie.

CAPTAIN
A team's leader.

DRAFT
An event that allows teams to choose new players coming into the league.

EXPANSION TEAM
A new team in a league, usually from a city that has not had a team in that league before.

FORWARD
A left wing, center, or right wing.

POWER PLAY
A situation in which one team has more players on the ice because an opposing player is serving a penalty.

RIVALS
Opposing players or teams that bring out the greatest emotion from fans and players.

TO LEARN MORE

BOOKS

Doeden, Matt. *G.O.A.T. Hockey Teams*. Minneapolis: Lerner Publications, 2021.

Duling, Kaitlyn. *Women in Hockey*. Lake Elmo, MN: Focus Readers, 2020.

Williamson, Ryan. *Nikita Kucherov: Hockey Superstar*. Burnsville, MN: Press Box Books, 2019.

MORE INFORMATION

To learn more about the Tampa Bay Lightning, go to **pressboxbooks.com/AllAccess**.

These links are routinely monitored and updated to provide the most current information available.

INDEX

Andreychuk, Dave, 18

Bradley, Brian, 14

Cirelli, Anthony, 26
Colton, Ross, 6

Esposito, Phil, 11–12

Fedotenko, Ruslan, 18

Gourde, Yanni, 8, 29

Hamrlik, Roman, 14
Hedman, Victor, 29

Johnson, Tyler, 20

Khabibulin, Nikolai, 18

Kontos, Chris, 13

Kucherov, Nikita, 20, 25

Lecavalier, Vincent, 14, 17

Palat, Ondrej, 20

Rhéaume, Manon, 12

Richards, Brad, 17

Savard, David, 6

Stamkos, Steven, 20, 22, 25, 29

Stillman, Cory, 17

Tortorella, John, 17

Vasilevskiy, Andrei, 7–8, 25–26, 29